Hiking Safely in Grizzly Country

MORE LESSONS LEARNED

Hiking Safely in Grizzly Country

More Lessons Learned

Tim Rubbert

RIVERBEND
PUBLISHING

All bear photos in this book were taken with
telephoto lenses using 6x to 10x magnification.
All photographs by Tim Rubbert unless otherwise noted.

Hiking Safely in Grizzly Country: More Lessons Learned
Copyright © 2016 by Tim Rubbert

Published by Riverbend Publishing, Helena, Montana

ISBN 13: 978-1-60639-095-5

Printed in the United States of America.

1 2 3 4 5 6 7 8 9 10 11 12 MG 26 25 24 23 22 21 20 19 18 17 16

Design by DD Dowden

RIVERBEND PUBLISHING®
P.O. Box 5833
Helena, MT 59604
1-866-787-2363
www.riverbendpublishing.com

To my nephew, Christopher Paul Nelson,
who lived three lifetimes in 30 years,
and to Jim Cole and Joseph Brady,
both of whom had more passion for the
great bear and its conservation than
anyone I have ever known.

ALSO BY TIM RUBBERT

Hiking with Grizzlies: Lessons Learned

CONTENTS

The female grizzly bear known as "Blaze,"
Yellowstone National Park.

Introduction

It has been ten years since I wrote my first book, *Hiking with Grizzlies: Lessons Learned.* Since then, I have hiked 20,000 more miles and experienced over 1,000 more grizzly bear sightings. Not surprisingly, I have learned more lessons. I have also had a lot of time to reflect on the beliefs that I held back then.

The purpose of this book is to use my experiences in the last ten-plus years to provide a basis for the reader to have more confidence about hiking safely in grizzly country. I also want to give an insight into what a grizzly bear is, and our place in the land this great bear calls home.

When people think about hiking in grizzly country, safety should be the number one priority. I will reiterate the same six principles that were emphasized in my first book, some to a lesser extent and others to a greater. I will also expand on topics I barely touched on, such as hiking alone. This book can be read in conjunction with my previous one. I want the reader to not only learn from my new experiences, but to see the evolution in my thinking about both old and new encounters.

The six principles that are the foundation of safe hiking in grizzly country are:
- Be able to recognize grizzly habitat.
- Be able to determine if a grizzly may be nearby.
- Make adequate noise.
- If a bear is encountered, freeze and remain calm.
- Judge how the bear is reacting to being in your presence.
- Carry and be able to use bear spray.

Of these six, making noise and carrying bear spray are the most important. If the reader remembers nothing else, these two safety procedures will make up for many miscues when hiking in grizzly country.

I have experienced much in the past ten years, and if there is one thing I have learned, it is the fact that I have a lot to learn. These new experiences have revealed subtle behavior traits that I had never noticed. These revelations have had a profound effect on some of my previous bear theories, most importantly those dealing with "habituated" grizzlies. The label "habituated" has usually implied something negative, such as bears that have learned to seek food associated with humans, but such food-conditioned bears are in a class by themselves. I now refer to wild grizzlies that generally accept the presence of humans as "tolerant" grizzlies.

It may not be people that cause a bear to become tolerant, nor is it some flaw in a grizzly that causes it to be near people. The grizzly, an unusually intelligent animal, will take advantage of opportunities it perceives as beneficial. For some bears, as will be discussed in this book, the presence of people may be beneficial. We are only now beginning to recognize and understand such behavior.

This is an important concept. Making noise while hiking doesn't necessarily mean you won't see a bear at close range. The main reason for making noise is to avoid surprising a bear at close range. Most maulings occur because the bear was surprised at a very close distance. Making noise increases the chances that you won't surprise a bear.

I do not believe it is always a natural response for a grizzly bear to run from people. If you are making adequate noise and you still run into a bear, more than likely it is a tolerant bear. This does not mean you should abandon safe hiking principles.

You should freeze and remain calm, and watch how the bear is reacting to your presence. A tolerant grizzly may look at you but will return to whatever it was doing before you came on the scene. Many tolerant bears may not acknowledge your presence, but believe me, they know you are there.

Of course, even normally tolerant bears have their limits. One situation where the bear may not be tolerant is when it is feeding on a carcass. In this case, hopefully, you have your can of bear spray out and ready to use.

As more and more people recreate in grizzly country, more bears may appear to be tolerant. This does not mean hiking and encounter strategies should be ignored. Always respect grizzlies no matter how or where you encounter them. Carry bear spray, have it readily available, and know how to use it. I have had to use bear spray in two extreme encounters. It worked both times. However, I do not want to put myself in a situation where I have to spray a bear again. I hope this book will give you enough information to avoid ever having to use it.

CHAPTER 1
CHARACTERISTICS OF GRIZZLY COUNTRY

If you are preparing to hike in grizzly country, it is important to learn the components that make up grizzly habitat. There are many areas in the western United States that still contain good habitat, but unfortunately, do not contain the number one component of grizzly country: the grizzly bear itself.

For this book I will only discuss the characteristics of places where grizzlies already exist or may in the future. For example, all of western Montana should be considered grizzly country. Even though some areas have not seen grizzlies for a hundred years, the possibility exists of running into one almost anywhere in western Montana. The same situation now applies to western Wyoming, Idaho, some portions of Washington, and most of Alaska. In Canada, the Yukon, the western portion of the Northwest Territories, western Alberta and most of British Columbia should be considered grizzly country.

What makes these areas special is that many of the people who live there accept the presence of the great bear as an integral part of the ecosystem. Many of these people want to live in the last "wild" places on earth.

Our attitudes will determine the survival of the grizzly as well as the continuing existence of wilderness. I would argue that the grizzly bear is not just a symbol of wilderness, but is actually the soul of wilderness. For me, wilderness is where grizzlies live. As I am writing this, I am witnessing a beautiful sunset over a federally designated wilderness area in Colorado. In my opinion, this is not real wilderness. There are no grizzlies in Colorado. It is, however, great grizzly habitat.

Most people would argue that it is poor grizzly habitat because there are too many people. I disagree. People didn't destroy the habitat; they destroyed the grizzly. They basically hunted down and killed every grizzly they could find. The food sources, the water, the cover, and the other characteristics of grizzly habitat are still there. It was the people's attitudes that determined the fate of the grizzly, not the loss of the habitat.

What really is grizzly country? It is some of the most spectacularly beautiful country on the planet. It is home not only to the grizzly, but to clean water, clear air, healthy forests, abundant vegetation, and other wildlife. It is in one word: exhilarating. It is accessible to people and for many it is home. It has always been home to both people and bears. Native Americans lived with the great bear for thousands of years. They respected and revered it. The bear was an intricate part of their lives and religion. It was, and is, a teacher. The grizzly has taught me incredible lessons of survival and tolerance. Every time I venture into grizzly country, I learn something new. In this context, we are able to explore the characteristics of grizzly country in a more insightful manner.

FOOD

The word "food" has so many implications in grizzly country. It is both a key to the bear's survival and at times the cause of its demise. Present-day people produce copious amounts of garbage. Sometimes they dispose of it properly, other times, not. A bear that gets into garbage or actually gets fed by people has the potential to become more than just a nuisance. Once a grizzly associates people with food rewards, it can become dangerous. Most grizzlies that get into garbage or are fed by humans end up being killed, either by wildlife officials trying to protect the public or illegally by people trying to protect their property. A common phrase in grizzly country is, "A fed bear is a dead bear." It is of upmost importance that anyone recreating or living in grizzly country properly dispose of garbage and secure food and other attractants away from bears.

Abundant, naturally occurring foods are the most important component of grizzly country. These take many forms. I still discover new sources every year. Grizzlies are omnivores. They eat both meat and vegetation. One of the main tenants of safe hiking is the ability to recognize prime grizzly foods. The following list and descriptions are certainly not all inclusive, but should give the reader a basis for determining the possibility of an encounter. Hikers should always check with local authorities to determine what the grizzlies in that area are feeding on.

Berries: These include huckleberries and blueberries, serviceberries, soap or buffalo berries, chokecherries, raspberries, elderberries, kinnikinnick (known as bear berry in Alaska), mountain ash, rose hip, and certainly others. Huckleberries and serviceberries are the main, but not only, berry sources in the Northern Continental Divide Ecosystem (NCDE) which includes Glacier National Park and the Bob Marshall Wilderness Complex in Montana. In Denali National Park in Alaska and in southwest Alberta, soapberries, also known as buffalo berries in some areas, are a main berry source.

The small berries of kinnikinnick, which exists from Denali to Grand Teton National Park in Wyoming, are of prime importance. I have seen grizzlies eat kinnikinnick in late fall when other berries were gone for the year and in early spring before other berries have appeared. **(See color photo 1)** The berry can winter very well under deep snow. Because of this ability, and its widespread distribution, it is one of the most important yet underrated bear foods.

Roots: Many plants have edible roots. These include, but are not limited to, glacier lily, spring beauty, biscuit root, clover, and hedysarum. Where I live, glacier lily and biscuit root are the primary roots in the spring. In the fall, hedysarum and glacier lily roots are usually a good food source. I have seen biscuit root also used as a food source in the Greater Yellowstone Ecosystem in the spring, and I have seen hedysarum used in Denali National Park in the middle of the summer. When determining whether grizzlies are eating any of these roots, you look for "diggings"—areas where the ground has been dug up. With their long claws and massive shoulder muscles, as evidenced by the unique shoulder hump, grizzlies can excavate large areas. Diggings of most roots are fairly obvious.

Other vegetation: Grizzlies eat above-ground parts of many plants. These include equisetum (horsetail), cow parsnip, dandelions, grasses, clover, sedge, bear flowers (which I have only seen in Denali), and the flowers of the glacier lily. I have never seen a grizzly eat cow parsnip after it flowers, but I have seen video of them doing so. In my experience, they prefer it during its early growth. Unlike diggings, sometimes it is difficult to see if a grizzly has eaten any of these plants. Therefore, if you see these plants, just assume a grizzly is in the area, especially in the spring when these plants are the most tender and nutritious.

Other animals: A grizzly will eat just about any dead animal including other bears and dead humans. The grizzly is a natural scavenger. The grizzly will also kill to eat. It can and will kill just about any animal from the size of a vole to a full-grown elk or moose. The smaller the animal, the faster the bear will consume it. The larger the animal, the better the chance that the bear will spend more time eating it, even sleeping on or near the carcass. In many cases grizzlies bury the carcasses of larger animals under a mound of dirt and vegetation. This lessens the odor and thus lessens the risk of other bears or scavengers finding this important food. Because large dead animals are fairly rare but so nutritionally valuable, bears will often aggressively defend carcasses from other scavengers and perceived threats, including people. When hiking, be alert for strong odors (especially the smell of rotting meat) and look for coyotes, wolves, ravens, eagles, magpies, and seagulls. Unusual concentrations of one or more of these species in a small area is a good indication that a carcass is nearby, perhaps with a grizzly bear ready to defend it. Either turn back or give these areas a very wide berth, making noise, having bear spray in hand, and taking the other safety measures in this book.

WATER

Grizzlies love water. They swim in it, play in it, drink it, fish in it, and even use it for traveling. For the grizzly, water is both a source of hydration and a way to cool off in hot weather. In grizzly country, water is always nearby. When water is scarce as in drought years, some water sources can attract many bears.

Snow is also used for both cooling and hydration. Many times I have seen bears using snow as a water source instead of bodies of water for no other reason than the snow was closer.

Grizzlies love to play in the snow. Many times you can see marks where grizzlies have slid down snow-covered slopes.

No matter the physical form of water, extra care should be taken near water sources. When you are hiking near waterfalls or rushing streams and rivers, you must make extra noise so that any nearby bear can hear you over the sound of water. Grizzlies may bed down in cool, shady wet areas. A grizzly lying on a snowfield may look like nothing more than a large rock.

COVER

I consider cover to be anything that can conceal a grizzly bear from sight. This includes both natural and man-made features. When vision is limited, special care must be taken. Making significant noise is absolutely required. The following types of cover are only a small part of what can be encountered in grizzly country.

Bushes: Bushes can be food sources like huckleberries or simply concealing plants like willows. In either case, they can be quite thick and large. I have seen huckleberry bushes four feet high and willows over my head. Even modest bushes are big enough to hide a sleeping grizzly or even one foraging. You may encounter large areas of dense bushes along waterways and hillsides, including avalanche chutes. I know people, including myself, that have walked right by grizzlies that were eating berries a few feet off the hiking trail. Of course, we were making noise so the bears knew we were there instead of being surprised, and they were tolerant bears that did not react negatively.

Thick forest or groups of trees: Grizzlies love to bed down in the shadows of trees, especially during the day.

These temporary places to rest and sleep are called "day beds." Grizzlies like the thick shade for both its cooling effect and its concealment. These areas are even more desirable when both water and food are nearby. Also, grizzlies may drag carcasses into nearby trees to gain more solitude.

Rocky areas: These areas include cliffs, steep hillsides, and boulder fields. I have seen grizzlies bedded down on the tops of cliffs above hiking trails where they were not visible from the trails. I have also seen bears feeding on berries that simply walked behind large rocks and disappeared. Climbers and anyone hiking near timberline should be aware of the potential for bears to be in rocky areas.

Sagebrush: Sagebrush is a rather unique cover. It usually grows in large open areas where good visibility seems to stretch for miles. Such areas are deceiving. My friend, Jim Cole, and I experienced the sighting of Jim's first Yellowstone grizzly in the middle of Hayden Valley in May 1994. Sagebrush is all over Hayden Valley. We were glassing with binoculars from one of the higher points in the valley when we spotted a grizzly in the sagebrush about 250 yards below us. It was digging—for what? We did not have a clue. As the grizzly moved off we decided to see what it had excavated. As we were hiking down the hillside from the east, we were able to keep our eye on the bear as it continued to move west. We thought we would be able to see the bear for a long time because it was traveling through this large, open expanse. We hiked a bit lower and immediately lost sight of the bear. We quickly realized the entire valley was made up of small dips and swells—all nearly hidden by the sagebrush that was two- to five-feet high. Thinking we could keep track of a bear in this environment was foolhardy. Bushwhacking called for much noise and deliberation.

We reached the digging area and still could not determine what was being dug. Only later when we talked to another bear observer did we learn that the grizzly was digging for pocket gophers and their caches of seeds, a prime spring food source for grizzlies. We learned lessons on this hike: (1) when looking for grizzlies, open areas can be deceptive, and (2) sagebrush areas can be prime grizzly habitat despite appearances to the contrary.

Tundra: In many ways tundra presents the same problem as sagebrush. In Alaska, especially, the vast open tundra areas are deceiving. The vegetation is anywhere from six inches tall to eight feet or more. Instead of sagebrush, you have grasses and dwarf bushes such as willow. Because of the vastness, it is hard to judge distances and thus the size of the vegetation. As in Hayden Valley, the tundra in Denali consists of rolling hills, swells, dips, and ridges. When Jim and I were there in 1994 conducting grizzly observations for the U.S. Biological Survey, we tried to hike on the ridges as they provided the best footing and views. We had radio telemetry equipment and we still lost sight of radio-collared bears. It reinforced the fact that open landscapes can still hide bears.

TRAVEL CORRIDORS

People have travel corridors. We generally know them as trails, sidewalks, streets, roads, highways, rail systems, etc. They make getting from point A to point B easier and quicker, using the least amount of energy.

Grizzlies use travel corridors for the same reasons. They use trails made by humans **(Photo 2)**, themselves, and by other animals. They use roads, both existing and abandoned, and they use railroad right-of-ways and power-line clearings. Of course they also use creeks, rivers, forest edges, ridge tops, lakes, and lake shores. You might say bears are like electricity: they both take the path of least resistance.

The result is that you can definitely run into a grizzly on a trail or road. I've done it numerous times. When many people see a grizzly on the trail, they immediately think they are being stalked. More than once I have had to tell hikers to calm down as I explained that the bears use trails for the same reasons we do. There have been many grizzlies killed on railroads and highways because they were using them for ease of travel. Forest edges and ridge tops provide similar ease of travel opportunities, but obviously with less risk. Anytime you use a geographic feature that makes your travel easier, it will make travel for a grizzly bear easier too. If a cleared trail makes it easier to hike through a maze of downed trees or heavy brush, bears will use it too. Special attention needs to be focused on these "bear ways."

I've tried to point out the basic aspects of grizzly country that need to be recognized in order to increase the chances of a safe journey. If you are aware of what a grizzly considers important, you have more knowledge to avoid surprise encounters—and you will learn more about this animal and the real wilderness.

CHAPTER 2
MAKE NOISE!

The best way to avoid encountering a grizzly is to make noise. Actually, that is not true. The best way to avoid encountering a grizzly is to stay out of grizzly country. However, many people would not even consider such an option. Some people visit grizzly country to see a grizzly, but most visitors simply want to experience the beauty and unique recreational opportunities such country provides. For those people, the thought of encountering a grizzly probably never enters their minds. Therefore, the first step in hiking safely in grizzly country is to become aware that the possibility exists—however small— that an encounter could occur. ***Making noise is the one tactic that offers the greatest protection against a negative encounter with a grizzly.***

Making noise will not guarantee that you will not run into a grizzly, but it will lessen the risk that you will surprise one at close range. Most maulings occur because the person basically walks right into a grizzly without any warning. The hiker ends up scaring the daylights out of the bear and the grizzly reacts instinctively to protect itself and/or its cubs. Making noise gives the bear a "heads up." If you are making appropriate noise you may never see the bear that has heard you coming. In many cases the grizzly runs away or "hides" until you have safely passed. In other cases the bear merely goes about its business such as eating berries or traveling.

The noise I usually make is loudly saying "hell-ooo," "yoo-hoo," or "yo." Sometimes I say "hey Booboo." Many hikers say "hey bear." The loudness and frequency varies, depending on the environmental conditions. Rushing water, wind, thick cover, and limited visibility usually dictate that I make louder and more frequent noise. Each hiker needs to use his or her own judgment. When in doubt, make more and louder noise.

When hiking alone I make noise on a fairly consistent basis. Since I believe that any encounter within 50 yards could turn into a serious situation, I make enough noise so that a bear can hear me from that distance.

If hiking with other people, especially three or more, the normal conversation generated is usually (but not always) enough to alert bears to your presence. Again, when in doubt, make noise.

Whistling is not recommended since marmots (also known as whistle pigs) whistle, and grizzlies eat marmots. Also, most "bear bells" are not loud enough. Cow bells would be loud enough, but if they are clanging all the time, your hearing of other things around you would be severely affected. In other words, I do not recommend any whistles or bells for making noise.

The following situations illustrated the effect of making appropriate noise.

Eastside Glacier National Park - August 2007

My sister, Debby Nelson, and I decided to take a short evening hike. My wife, Suzi, and I had done this same hike earlier that day and saw a mother grizzly and yearling cub high above the trail. I felt we would have a good chance to see them again because the serviceberries in that area were abundant. As we started up the trail we ran into a hiker coming down the trail. He stated that he had just seen a mother and cub further up the trail. We continued on, making noise as we went.

Since there were intermittent thick bushes next to the trail, I was making louder, more frequent noise. I was also hiking with my bear spray in my hand with the safety off. We climbed a steep portion of the trail. It began to level out when I caught a flash of brown approaching the trail about 20 feet to my left. I knew it was a bear even though I did not stop to look directly at it. I kept hiking at the same speed until I felt I was a safe distance away. I stopped and turned to see a mother grizzly and cub-of-the-year coming up to the trail. Debby, who was behind me as we hiked up the steep portion, had already stopped as she had seen the bears come towards the trail in front of her.

It was then, after seeing that the mother bear was not agitated with our presence, that I took out my camera and started taking pictures **(Photo 3)**. The mother and cub crossed the trail between my sister and me and moved above the trail where they started eating the ripe serviceberries **(Photos 4 and 5)**. As we watched and photographed the bears, more people came up and down the trail. Nobody freaked out. Some people took pictures or simply watched. Others continued hiking. The grizzlies slowly worked their way through the berry patches above the trail until they disappeared over a ridge.

I believe the key to this safe and amazing encounter was the fact that we were making appropriate noise. The mother grizzly knew we were coming. We did not surprise them even though we encountered them at very close range. In addition, everyone that was fortunate to see this family group acted in a responsible and calm manner, and the bears acted in a very tolerant way.

Eastside Glacier National Park - June 2008

I took an early morning hike to a beautiful lake. I was alone and all signs indicated I was the first person on the trail. The sun was to my back as I entered a semi-open area along the lakeshore. I had been making noise the whole way and continued to do so. I had taken this route two days earlier and had seen two grizzlies. One was a large male (it was mating season) and the other was what I presumed to be a female. The female had been digging glacier lily roots near the lakeshore in an area covered in thick brush. Making noise was a necessity. I also carried my bear spray in hand the entire way.

I reached my destination without seeing any bears. I sat down in a fairly open area to glass the nearby mountainsides and soak up the warm morning sun. It was still fairly early. I decided to hike back to the trailhead and head home. I continued to make noise on the way back. I learned a long time ago that just because you do not see any bears on the way in, doesn't mean you won't see any on the way back. Also, the corollary is that just because you don't see any bears, doesn't mean there are none in the area.

About halfway back as I rounded a sharp turn in the trail, I looked up and saw a grizzly walking right towards me on the trail. It looked like the female I had seen a couple of days earlier. If I backed up, I would lose sight of her. I had two options: (1) I could hold my ground and hope she would either turn back or she would leave the trail and go around me, or (2) I could get off the trail and hope she would walk by me and keep going. Since there was an open, albeit slightly steep slope for me to get off the trail, I did so.

I was able to get about 30 yards off the trail. The bear continued walking down the trail to where I had just been. Since she showed no sign of aggression, I decided to take some pictures. You can see that she kept her eye on me as she passed **(Photo 6)**. When she got a safe distance farther down the trail, I climbed back to it. I took a photo as she gave me one last glance **(Photo 7)**. She then disappeared around the corner into thick brush where I presumed she dug glacier lilies. At this point I continued back to the trailhead and my vehicle. Before I left for home I stopped at the ranger station and left a note for the local bear ranger letting him know what happened. I thought he might want to "post" the trail so other hikers would know of the bear on or near the trail.

By making noise I believe the grizzly was alerted to my presence. I did not surprise her when I rounded the corner on the trail. I felt that since she knew I was on the trail, she was able to remain calm. I also believe that moving below the trail and giving her room to go past made her more tolerant of my presence.

Eastside Glacier National Park - August 2013

I took a hike in the same area described above. This time I was hiking with Shane Conner, a wildlife biologist and fellow bear enthusiast. It was a morning hike on a clear, beautiful day. We were not the first ones on the trail. We knew this because we met a couple on their way back. They stated that they just observed a grizzly near the trail a few hundred yards ahead of us. Because of the time of year and the fact that I saw many ripe serviceberry patches near this trail a couple of days earlier, I figured the bear was in the area to eat the berries.

Shane and I continued on the trail, making noise and with our bear sprays in hand. I was in the lead. We hiked deliberately, inspecting every nook and cranny along the trail. We reached our destination without seeing or hearing the bear. When bears are eating berries they sometimes can be heard moving through the brush. They aren't trying to be quiet. We stopped and glassed open areas without spotting any bears. After a few more minutes we decided to head back to the trailhead.

As we hiked back we were just as deliberate as on the way in. We continued to make as much noise and still had our bear sprays out. This time Shane was in the lead. As we passed a group of serviceberry bushes I heard some brush move a little behind and to my left. Without breaking stride or stopping I took a quick glance towards the sound and was slightly surprised to see a grizzly about 10 feet off the trail, eating serviceberries. I turned towards Shane and said, "Hey Mono (his nickname) you just walked right by a grizzly." Of course, so did I. If that bear had not made any noise, or if I had not heard it, we would have walked past without seeing it, even though it was only a few feet away.

We hiked a little farther, stopped, and turned around just as the grizzly stepped onto the trail and walked away from

Photo A

us. The grizzly then moved above the trail into a large open area and we walked back up the trail to take more photos as the grizzly fed on berries and slowly made its way up the mountainside. **(Photo A, opposite page)**

Once again, making noise was the key to a safe encounter. The grizzly remained calm and was totally tolerant of our presence. In all of my years of hiking in grizzly country I have only had (thank God!) two severe encounters. Both could be directly attributable to the lack of making appropriate noise.

CHAPTER 3
CARRY BEAR SPRAY!

I cannot overemphasize the importance of carrying bear spray. Since the development and availability of bear spray in the early 1980s, the majority—if not all—of the people killed by grizzlies were not carrying it. I know of no incident where a person who was able to successfully deploy bear spray was seriously mauled or killed. Of course this implies that one must not only carry bear spray, but must have it readily available and know how to use it. Carrying bear spray in the bottom of your pack, for example, is worthless. It must be in hand or available in an instant. Grizzlies are unbelievably quick.

There are at least four bear sprays on the market that are registered with and approved by the Environmental Protection Agency. Only use bear sprays with such approval. The EPA registration number will be on the can.

I recommend bear sprays with a spray distance of at least 25 feet and a spray duration of at least six seconds. Without such properties, I probably would not have experienced a successful outcome when I sprayed the grizzly that attacked Jim Cole in Glacier, described later in this chapter. The only bear spray that I know of that meets these specifications is Counter Assault Bear Spray, which I have been carrying since 1985. I cannot recommend other bear sprays since I have not used any others.

All bear sprays work the same way. The trigger is protected by a safety cover to prevent accidental discharge. Many people, if they have not practiced, cannot remove the safety. ***The most***

important thing to learn is how to remove the safety quickly and effectively. Depressing the trigger and spraying is similar to operating other household and industrial propellants, so people usually have some experience with that feature.

The best way to learn how to use bear spray is to practice with training canisters from Counter Assault and other manufacturers. Training cans should only be used outside, as the propellant can be irritating to the eyes and throat. If no training canister can be obtained, then I recommend using a can of real bear spray. With the wind at your back in an open area far away from any structures, cars, pets and people, flip off the safety and fire a short burst. Using a real can in this manner will give you an idea of how to remove the safety and see the spray pattern, and still have enough contents in the can to use while hiking. (Bear sprays have expiration dates; if you need to buy a new can, use the old can for practice.) It is important to remember that the spray disperses and will not be visible after a short time, but it can still cause irritation.

I have had to use bear spray in two extreme situations. I emphatically attest to its efficacy.

Glacier National Park - September 29, 1993
Jim Cole and I started on a 25-mile day hike at 7:30 a.m. on a beautiful fall morning. Our destination was the Fifty Mountain area 12.5 miles away. We reached the area about noon. We had not seen fresh grizzly sign on our way in, but here were numerous fresh diggings of glacier lily roots. We ate lunch and glassed the open areas for grizzlies without any luck. We thought they might be bedded down on the warm fall afternoon. At 2 p.m. we decided to head back.

Jim led the way. I stopped and scanned open areas wherever there was a good view, then caught up with Jim until

PHOTO 1

PHOTO 2

PHOTO 3

PHOTO 4

PHOTO 5

PHOTO 6

PHOTO 7

PHOTO 8

PHOTO 9

PHOTO 10

PHOTO 11

PHOTO 12

and had breakfast, consisting of dry food, along with a sports drink in my water bottle.

I continued glassing. At about 10:40 a.m. I heard something behind me. I quickly looked around and came face to face with a mule deer doe that was watching me from about 20 feet away. A little later I decided to move to a higher elevation where I could see more territory.

I stood up and started packing to leave. As I bent down to put my food bag into my pack, I noticed a flash of brown out of the corner of my eye. I looked up and saw a female grizzly with a yearling cub coming around a small group of trees about 20 yards away. She saw me at almost the same instant, and she immediately charged!

My only thought was, "I hope that can of bear spray that I put on the ground next to me is at my feet when I look down." I had another can of spray in a holster on my pack belt, but knew I didn't have time to lift up the pack and get that can. I looked down and there, thank God, was the can I had placed on the ground. I reached down and grabbed it. As I pulled off the safety I said in a loud, low voice, "NOoo...!" I intended to say "NO, don't come any closer," but "NO" was all I got out.

The two grizzlies promptly stopped and stood up. The cub did exactly what its mother did. They were both huffing. I actually thought it was kind of cute. It was as if the cub was trying to be a tough guy, saying, "Oh boy, Mom, we're going to nail this guy." It was a ridiculous thought, but I have learned that in life-threatening situations, when things are happening very fast, the mind does not operate in the "normal" fashion.

The standing bears were about 20 feet away. I could clearly see the female's six swollen teats. She came down on all fours towards me and I instantly triggered a short burst of bear spray at her face. The cloud of spray headed straight towards her, but in the strong wind (the wind had come up while I had been sitting on the cliff) the spray made a 90-degree turn before it got to her. Luckily, the "whoosh" sound from the can and the red cloud of spray startled both bears and again they slammed on the brakes.

Both grizzlies started moving laterally to my right. As they were moving, I glanced down the cliff. All of a sudden I realized I could climb down it. In all my previous visits to this cliff, I never thought it could be climbed, but now a few, small, possible footholds looked like a stairway to me. So I started to climb down, all the while facing the bears. There is no guarantee that bear spray will work 100 percent of the time. If it didn't work this time, I was going to bail off the cliff. However, I really didn't want to abandon my pack because there was food in it, and I was afraid the bears would get into it with dire consequences for them and possibly other hikers in the future.

The mother grizzly came towards me again. About 10 feet away she stopped and stood up. Now I had to look up at her because I had already moved down the cliff to the top of my knees. I wasn't going to wait for her to come down. I triggered the spray and this time, because of the short distance and favorable wind direction, the spray hit her directly in the face. In a flash, she and her cub were gone.

I could hear her huffing and puffing as they ran towards the trail. Unfortunately, they were headed in the same direction I had to go! I climbed on top of the cliff, gathered my things, and without delay started towards the trail. I wanted to get out of there. I pulled out my other can of bear spray and took off the safety. I walked deliberately and alertly with a can of bear spray in each hand and yelling, "Yo bear! Hey bear!" I did not see the grizzlies again as I reached the trail and hiked to the nearest park facility to report the encounter.

This incident shows that there are different ways encounters can occur. In the incident with Jim, humans "ran" into a grizzly. In this episode, grizzlies "ran" into a human. But both incidents had one main factor in common: the humans didn't make enough noise to alert the bears that humans were there. I firmly believe that both encounters could have been avoided with proper noise.

However, in the last incident I'm not sure that making constant or loud noises while sitting in a prime wildlife viewing area is conducive to the well-being of the animals being observed. A better tactic in such a situation would be to stay more alert and look all around on a consistent basis. Almost all of my time was spent focused on the valley below me and not behind or to the sides of me. It was fortunate that I had a can of bear spray on the ground next to me. It shows that bear spray must be readily available to be used effectively.

As stated previously, since the first incident, I now carry two cans of bear spray on my pack belt. **Photo B** shows me with my typical day-hiking set up. Notice that my two cans of spray are in front, on my pack belt, where they can be easily reached. They are in the same place when I wear my typical backpacking or long day-hiking arrangement. I often carry one can in my hand with the safety off, especially when hiking alone or in tight spots with limited visibility. **Photos C and D** show how I do this (these photos were taken by my wife, Suzi). Obviously, one has to be very careful not to accidentally discharge the spray when carrying it this way.

I want everyone who hikes in grizzly country to carry and know how to properly use bear spray. Not only is it important for one's own safety, but it can also save the lives of grizzlies by

Photo B

(left) photo C
(right) photo D

preventing serious or deadly maulings of people. In such cases, authorities usually feel the necessity to kill the "offending" bear even though it is usually the victim's fault for not following safe hiking protocols. Employing safe hiking strategies and tactics as presented in this book will, hopefully, help people avoid situations where they actually have to use bear spray. I never want to be in a situation where I have to use it again. It is not fun.

CHAPTER FOUR
HIKING ALONE

Hiking alone is not the recommended way of traveling through grizzly country. Hiking alone is rife with potential hazards and risks. Two of the biggest risks anywhere, not just in grizzly country, are getting lost and getting injured. Also, in grizzly country, there is no one to help you make noise or look for bears. The exception might be a popular trail that gets a lot of hiking traffic. Do not count on a cell phone to call for help. Much of grizzly country has no cell phone service. If you have a problem with a grizzly, you could be on your own. However, even with all these risks, hiking alone can be rewarding if you do it in a safe manner.

I hike alone. I will hike with others whenever possible, but since I hike almost every day, when most normal people are working, I often end up going alone. I do not consider this dangerous because I follow safe hiking practices. When you hike alone you must pay attention, think about what you are doing, and make more noise. You have to stay focused. As a result of hiking alone, I have seen many incredible things that I may not have seen had I been in a group of hikers. The following situations shed some light on the risks and rewards of hiking alone.

Yellowstone National Park - June 2008
It was the middle of elk calving season. I started on the trail at about 7:30 a.m., hiking to an open ridge where cow elk had been seen. About halfway up in a small open area between two

groups of trees, I caught a flash of something brown moving down the sagebrush hillside about 150 yards ahead of me. It was a small elk calf running down the hill with a grizzly in hot pursuit and with the mother elk and a coyote on the heels of the bear. This was amazing. I have witnessed both grizzlies and black bears killing elk calves, but only from the road.

The grizzly caught the calf in a second. Death was instant. I watched intently as the cow elk and coyote circled the bear. The grizzly was already beginning to tear into the calf. It was then that I decided to take out my camera and start taking photos. The bear had looked at me; it was aware of my presence. The distance between us was great enough that I believed the bear did not consider me a threat. Soon the bear's nose was red with blood (**Photo 8**). After a few minutes I wanted to continue my hike but the trail went closer to the bear. I did not want to get any closer, so I decided to bushwhack around the grizzly. I was slightly downhill from the bear. As I bushwhacked, I gained elevation and was soon above the grizzly. The bear looked up right at me and made a step in my direction. She, whom I later learned was a five-year-old female, was not happy. She probably thought I was either a threat or I was competing for the calf. I instantly froze and in a calm, soothing voice said, "What a good bear, what a pretty bear." She stopped, but kept looking at me. I slowly retreated downhill the exact way I had come up. As I started downhill she went back to eating. I went back to the area where I had been, and she continued to eat.

After about twenty minutes, two hikers came up the trail to me. When the bear now saw three of us, she picked up the dead calf and carried it into a group of trees away from us. There she continued to eat. I felt it was a good time to continue my hike to the open ridge. Once again I went around her, but was now far enough away that she did not even pay attention. About two hours later I came back the same way. She was just finishing consuming the calf. As I came down, she left the carcass and moved up the ridge where I had just been.

There is one thing I should not have done. I should not have tried to go around her the first time. I felt that I was at a safe distance, but she did not feel the same way. At least I kept my eyes on her in order to watch her reaction to my movements. The second I saw that she may be agitated, I froze. This calmed down the bear and I was able to retreat. In hindsight, I should have remained where I first saw her or should have hiked back down to the trailhead. When hiking alone, risks are magnified. The right decisions need to be made.

Glacier National Park - Eastside - June 2010

I started alone down a popular trail about 9 a.m. I passed many hikers and knew there were more ahead of me. As I approached a cliff area, I noticed a small group of people looking up. When I asked what they were looking at, they pointed into the cliffs at a mother grizzly with three cubs that were born earlier that year (known as cubs-of-the-year). I took out my binoculars and saw three little brown bundles of fur. Mother grizzlies with three cubs of any age are not common in Glacier. I was happy with this sighting. Soon the other people left and I moved off the trail to get a better angle of view. The bears were about 250 yards above me. I took out my camera and started taking pictures.

The bears were grazing on lush green grass in small flat areas interspersed in the band of cliffs. The mom and two of the cubs went up a large crack in the cliff face. The third cub kept grazing. The little cub finally realized that his mom and siblings were gone when they appeared directly above him on top of a 20-foot, almost shear rock face. The baby bear panicked and started climbing straight up **(Photo 9)**. I wish I would have had a video camera. I did not know if the little one could make it, but after a couple of minutes it successfully climbed to the top where the mother grizzly was patiently waiting **(Photo 10)**.

I had never seen anything like this. It was a completely safe situation for anyone watching. If I had refused to hike that day because I was alone, I would have missed this magical event. This mother and her three cubs would be regular visitors on the trails in this area over the next two years. She will be discussed in the chapter "Tolerant Grizzlies." I was lucky to see this family group near the beginning of their lives together.

Glacier National Park - Eastside - Early June 2013

It was about 8 a.m. on a sunny morning. I was driving a road looking for bears. Every now and then I would stop to look at distant open areas with my binoculars. I stopped again to look at an avalanche chute across a large body of water. I had looked at this area many times over the years and had never seen anything. This time, to my surprise, there were two young grizzlies "play" mating high up in the avalanche chute. It was, after all, mating season. I knew these two bears from seeing them a few times before. They had been together the previous fall and this spring. The female was a three-year-old and had a radio ear tag. We (the people who had previously seen them) figured that the male was either three or four years old. Since a hiking trail crossed the bottom of the chute, I decided to hike the trail to get a better view. The chute was about a mile from the trailhead and it took me about 25 minutes to reach it. I made noise the whole way and hiked with my bear spray out with the safety clip off.

The bears would be out of sight until I got within about 100 yards of the chute.

As I got close, I looked up the chute and did not see the bears. Then I looked straight ahead and saw the male on the trail about 60 yards ahead of me. The young female was in the chute about twenty yards above the line of trees. It was then that I heard some twigs snap behind me and to my right. I thought it was the female coming towards the trail through the trees and heavy brush. As I turned my head towards the sound, I was totally dumbfounded to see a very large, dark male grizzly walking right by me 10 feet away. I instinctively froze. What else could I do? Time seemed to stand still. All I could do was stand there with my mouth agape as I followed this large grizzly with my eyes. (**Photo E**)

At this point, I had no idea where the young grizzlies went. The "big boy" had my full attention. This large male ended up in a lush meadow right next to the water. I turned around

Photo E

and hiked back to the trailhead. I never saw the young bears again that day. The large dark male was known as "Buster." I had seen him earlier that year, but only at a distance. Buster had, without me knowing it, followed me down the trail. I soon realized the implications of what had happened. All my attention had been in front of me. I was not even thinking about behind me. From that day on, I stop much more often and look behind as I hike. Of course, I am not sure what I would have done if I had looked behind me that day. Since I had gotten a good look at him, I estimated his weight at 500 pounds. That means that in the fall he could have been a 700-pound bear—among the largest in the ecosystem. I have always said that large males like to keep track of what is going on in their territory. Most of the time you will never see them. The exception is during mating season.

This was a very close encounter, one that I would not want to experience again. I was alone. I had my bear spray out, and Buster was only ten feet away. Fortunately, he exhibited no signs of aggression. There was no reason to spray him and it would have been wrong to do so. Why would I want to aggravate a huge grizzly only ten feet away from me? There are definitely times to use bear spray; this was not one of them. The outcome of this encounter was as good as it could be. I am not sure if hiking with other people would have changed it. It is possible another member of the party could have panicked. In that type of situation, hiking alone might be preferable. You need to know who you hike with and they need to know how to react in an encounter. Everyone I hike with knows how to remain calm in encounter situations.

In hindsight, I never should have been on this hike. I broke one of my own safe hiking admonishments: keep your eyes on the bear(s). The minute I left the road, I lost sight of the two young bears. I really had no idea where they would be when I got to the avalanche chute. I was taking an unnecessary risk. One needs to reduce risks in grizzly country, not increase them.

Glacier National Park - October 2014

There was construction under way near the Many Glacier Hotel, so the trailhead I wanted was not accessible by car. I had to hike about two miles around Swiftcurrent Lake to reach it. Since I planned to go all the way to the head of Cracker Lake, it would be a 16-mile day.

I wanted to get to Cracker Lake to see if any grizzlies were eating hedysarum in the large open areas around the lake. After reaching the trailhead, I hiked about four miles without incident. As I approached a small bridge crossing a creek, I noticed a young couple with backpacks coming my way. I figured they must have camped overnight at Cracker Lake.

I asked them if that was the case. They acknowledged that they had, and that they had seen two grizzlies the previous evening, digging. They also stated they had just spooked a grizzly about a half mile further up the trail. It had run uphill into the brush and disappeared. I thanked them for the information and continued up the trail. I noted they both carried bear spray.

I continued hiking, knowing there might be as many as three grizzlies, maybe more, in the area. My hiking goal or strategy did not change. I knew that I could encounter grizzlies on any hike in the Many Glacier area. A bit further up the trail, as I rounded a corner, I saw a grizzly on the trail about forty yards ahead of me. It was looking directly at me. I froze and watched this bear's reaction. It was calm. I was calm. I softly talked to the bear as I reached for my camera. I took a couple of photos **(Photo F)** before the bear turned to my left and disappeared uphill into heavy cover. I waited a minute and then continued hiking. When I reached Cracker Lake there were fresh diggings of hedysarum, probably from the night before, all over the open areas. Some were within 100 yards of the campground. I glassed the entire area without seeing any grizzlies. As I hiked back, I thought about a number things, all the while making appropriate noise. If I had not met the couple, I still would have done the exact same things. I might have been surprised to see the grizzly on the trail, but I would have reacted the same way. As stated earlier, I knew I had a good chance to see grizzlies on this hike. The hike and encounter also validated my hiking strategy when hiking alone: Make noise and carry bear spray readily accessible. I carry my spray in hand with the safety clip off. I feel comfortable doing this, but be careful not to spray yourself or anyone else, especially if you trip or fall.

Photo F

Glacier National Park - Eastside - May 2015

A good friend of mine, wildlife biologist Shane Conner, and I decided to spend a couple of days on the east side of Glacier hiking numerous drainages looking for grizzly diggings, tracks, scat, and other signs, and in the process perhaps seeing a grizzly.

We took one trail to get above the valley floor. We glassed the entire area without spotting anything and started hiking back. About halfway down we reached a trail junction. Since we wanted to cover as much of the area as possible, we decided to take a different way back. As we reached a lake we noticed that the footbridge across a decent-sized creek had not been installed for the season. We did not want to wade the creek, so we turned back.

We had passed a horse trail before we came to the creek. As we came to it again, we decided to hike back on it. It soon became quite muddy with much standing water. Shane decided to turn back. I decided to keep going. We would meet each other at our vehicles, if not sooner on the trail.

As I continued down the horse trail I noticed fairly fresh grizzly tracks coming from the opposite direction. They appeared to be those of a large male, maybe Buster. I kept going. I was making noise and, of course, had my bear spray out. I was now, after all, hiking alone. A little bit further I came around a corner and there was a grizzly on the trail about 25 yards in front of me. It had heard me coming and was looking right at me. The scene was eerily similar to the one I had experienced the previous fall on the Cracker Lake trail.

Once again, I froze. This time, however, the bear did not seem calm. At first I thought it might be a small adult female with a cub, but I could not see much behind the bear because of heavy brush. I soon realized it was a lone young bear. I was thinking about getting out my camera, but the bear started to move its lower jaw up and down. This was not necessarily a sign of aggression, but it was at least a sign of agitation. I forgot about taking pictures. I started to talk to the bear in soft tones, "Oh, what a good bear. . . oh, what a pretty bear." The bear seemed to relax. It walked off the trail and slowly made its way around me. As soon as the bear was about 50 yards to my right, I continued down the trail, keeping my eye on it and continuing to talk in a soft and calm manner until the bear was out of sight. As I hiked, I noticed the bear's tracks in the mud. They appeared to be the size of a two-year-old bear. When I reached the main hiking trail a few minutes later, I followed it to the east. The young grizzly's tracks had originated about a mile further down. Bears use hiking trails.

I finally met Shane at the parking lot. We talked about what had happened. We agreed that taking a picture in my situation was not worth the risk. Making noise, having bear spray, and being able to freeze and remain calm when the situation calls for it are three of the basic tenets of hiking safely in grizzly country, whether you are alone or not.

If you hike alone, let someone know where you are going and when you will be back. Leave a note on your car if you need to. If you are afraid of grizzlies or you cannot not adhere to safe hiking strategies, do not hike alone in grizzly country.

Recently I have started carrying a Personal Locator Beacon, PLB for short. This device can be used to either send a pre-programmed message to someone (my wife, for example) or send an S.O.S. I have mine set up to send a preset message to my wife through email stating that everything is fine. This way I can send a reassuring message when I am out of cell-phone range for a long time. The S.O.S. message is sent to an organization specially dedicated to alerting the proper authorities. It is to be used only in life threatening situations. Both messages are sent through satellites that automatically record your exact location. The use of this device requires an annual subscription. Like bear spray, I feel it is better to have it and not need it than to need it and not have it. Hopefully, I will never have to use the S.O.S. message. In any case, it provides a special means of communication, especially when hiking alone and/or bushwhacking.

CHAPTER 5
BUSHWHACKING

Bushwhacking refers to hiking "off trail." This is not a recommended way of travel in any situation, let alone in grizzly country. Downfall (downed trees), slippery rocks and logs, holes, dips, cliffs, water hazards, heavy brush, etc. can make hiking not only extremely difficult, but also very dangerous. If anything happens, getting help can be problematical at best.

When you throw in the presence of grizzly bears, the potential for negative outcomes increases. Therefore, risk-reward analyses need to be seriously made. I have been to incredible places that could only be reached by bushwhacking. On some of these travels I have also run into dangerous situations. The following experiences illustrate some of the many dangers one could encounter while bushwhacking.

Yellowstone National Park - Early May, 2007
Jim Cole and I had been driving the park roads while we waited for the arrival of Sabrina Leigh, a young lady who had recently become interested in the ecology of grizzly bears. It was Sabrina's first visit to Yellowstone and we wanted her to be able to safely observe her first Yellowstone grizzlies. After overcoming some serious car problems, Sabrina finally arrived. The road scenario was not turning out to be very productive. We decided to take a hike in Hayden Valley. Even though we would be bushwhacking, we felt that the open vistas of the valley offered the best chances of seeing a grizzly at a safe distance.

From the road, Hayden Valley looks like it would be an easy place to hike and spot bears. However, as stated in previous chapters, looks can be deceiving. Hayden Valley is primarily a sagebrush landscape containing many small dips, knolls, ridges, low hills, and islands of trees. It is great bear country. It is imperative that one make noise and have bear spray readily accessible. Jim and I had hiked this particular section of the valley many times. We were well aware of the risks and related these to Sabrina before we started. Sabrina was an experienced hiker, but she was new to Yellowstone.

We started about 2:30 in the afternoon from a pullout along the road. We were taking the easiest route we knew. It also afforded the best views without venturing more than a mile from the road on a four-mile, cross-country loop. In addition to grizzlies, one of the unique things about Yellowstone are its many thermal features. Our planned route would basically circle around some of these very interesting—and possibly dangerous—formations. Another thing that makes Yellowstone different from any other national park are the herds of free-roaming bison. Most people don't realize how huge and fast these animals are. As a matter of fact, I am more concerned with running into bison at close range than a grizzly. We were all on constant alert for the many possible hazards we could encounter.

About 2.5 miles into our hike, we were going around some thermal features. We were making appropriate noise. We were all carrying bear spray. Jim was in the lead when he suddenly blurted, "There's a grizzly!" I looked up and saw the bear about 150 yards in front of us. We stopped, stood still, and watched the young bear. The grizzly stopped and watched us. The grizzly was fairly easy to spot because (1) it was on top of a small ridge and (2) the sagebrush was only about a foot high. **(Photo G)** Different terrain characteristics, such as higher sagebrush, could have made the grizzly much harder or even impossible to see.

After watching us for a moment, the grizzly ambled to the north and disappeared over the ridge. We continued our hike on the planned route without seeing any more bears and without further incident. We had followed safe hiking procedures even though we were bushwhacking. We were all glad that we were able to safely see this bear. It definitely made the hike worthwhile.

Glacier National Park - August, 2007

My sister, Debby Nelson, had been working at one of the park hotels for a good portion of the summer. She was fortunate to have hiked many of the trails near the hotel. She was also fortunate to have observed many grizzlies. On this particular

Photo G

day we decided to do a hike I had done a few times before. A good portion of the 12-mile hike would involve bushwhacking, including some cliff climbing. Debby was more than willing to attempt this endeavor because of the special opportunities it offered for viewing wildlife, especially grizzlies.

We started about 7 a.m. It had been a dry summer and several large wildfires were burning in northwest Montana. The rising sun produced a reddish hue in the smoky air. After about a mile and a half on a well-traveled hiking trail, we started hiking upwards on an old game trail. We soon encountered heavy brush and thick forest. Huckleberry bushes with ripe berries were interspersed throughout the area. Making noise was essential. We both had bear spray. I had one can in my hand with the safety off.

The going was slow because of the limited visibility and steep, rough terrain. After about 20-30 minutes we broke into an area below a band of reddish cliffs. I looked up and much to my surprise and delight I saw a mother grizzly and a yearling cub on top of one of the rock outcrops, studying us. She no doubt heard us coming. We froze and watched her reaction to us, which was basically the same as our reaction to her. After realizing we were not a threat to them, they started to move downhill towards an area of small trees surrounded by huckleberry bushes. We remained still and watched them. The bears soon disappeared into the thick cover.

We now had a dilemma. The game trail went into the thick brush the grizzlies had just entered. There was no way we were going there. We talked about our options. We decided to detour up and around. Because of the abundance of huckleberries, we figured the grizzly family was partaking of the delicious fruit. We basically headed up to where the bears had been when we first saw them. The hillside there was quite open and offered us a direct line of sight into the cover where the grizzlies had disappeared.

We continued to make noise as we circled the area. I could now see where the game trail continued on the other side of the thick cover. We had to go slightly downhill and cross a small ravine to get back on the game trail. As I crossed the ravine, I looked down and was slightly surprised to see the mother grizzly and her cub taking a refreshing dip in a small pool of water.

Once more we froze, remained calm, and watched how the grizzlies reacted to our presence. Once again, the mother showed no sign of agitation. I took out my camera and took some photos (**Photos 11 and 12**). In photo 11 the mother looks like she may be roaring. Actually she is yawning. The cub moved out of view while the mother grizzly laid back down in the small pool. Debby and I slowly continued our climb, all the while making noise (there could have been other bears in the area) and keeping an eye on the two bears now well below us. The mother eventually got out of the water and followed her cub into the huckleberry bushes.

We continued our hike without further incident. Once again the sighting of grizzlies made it an exceptional experience. I believed we followed safe hiking procedures, except for the fact that we were bushwhacking. The most dangerous portion of the bushwhacking was climbing some cliffs we encountered after we left the grizzlies. Making noise, carrying bear spray, and knowing how to react when a grizzly is encountered can lessen the risks of bushwhacking but cannot eliminate them.

BUSHWHACKING GONE WRONG
Hayden Valley, Yellowstone National Park - May 23, 2007
I knew Jim Cole was in Yellowstone. I had talked to him the

previous day. I had just spent the night up the North Fork of the Flathead River across from the western boundary of Glacier National Park. I started hiking up a gated road in the Whitefish Mountain Range west of the river about 7:30 a.m. I was hiking alone so I had my bear spray out with the safety off and I was making noise. My destination was some avalanche chutes about 7.5 miles up the road where I hoped to catch a glimpse of a grizzly. Unbeknownst to me, Jim Cole, at about 8:30 a.m., would begin a bushwhack through Hayden Valley, also hoping to get a glimpse of a grizzly.

As I neared my destination, I studied the large avalanche chutes on the north side of the road. It was a beautiful, clear day so I had good visibility all the way to the top of the ridge where the chutes originated. After a few minutes of glassing, I continued up the road. A few minutes later I heard and saw an airplane circling above the avalanche chutes. I reversed direction and went back toward the slide areas. The plane soon left, but it had piqued my curiosity. It had been my experience that circling planes in remote areas usually indicate some sort of wildlife study, survey, or actual sighting. Considering the area, I felt a radio-collared grizzly could have been the object of the plane's attention.

I again reached the bottom of the chutes, looked up with my binoculars, and immediately saw a grizzly about 800 yards away in some thick brush that had not yet leafed out. It was about 10 a.m. I soon saw another grizzly, then another. It was a radio-collared mother with a pair of two-year-old cubs. I observed them for about 30 minutes. I even saw them nurse, then they moved into thick cover and disappeared. I headed home. It had been a very rewarding hike. I got home about 4 p.m., related the details of my trip to my wife, had dinner, took a shower, and went to bed.

About 3 a.m. we were awakened by the phone ringing. As probably with most people, a call in the middle of the night was a very rare occurrence. I jumped out of bed and answered the phone. It was a good friend of Jim's who lived in Colorado. I knew something bad had happened. The friend said Jim had been severely mauled by a grizzly the previous morning (while I was hiking in the Whitefish Range). He was now in a hospital in Idaho Falls. I did not go back to bed. Suzi got up and made coffee.

A few hours later I started to make phone calls. I needed to let friends know what happened, and I wanted to find out if there was any information about the attack. There were scattered reports on the internet, but the stories were just rumor or conjecture. Most of the people I talked to could not believe Jim had gotten mauled again. Has anyone ever been mauled twice by grizzly bears?

I started to get first-hand reports of Jim's condition. A friend at the hospital said Jim was heavily sedated after undergoing many hours of surgery to reconstruct his face, which had been almost completely torn off. Jim's friend did not know any details of the attack. Only later on Saturday, May 26, when Jim called me after regaining suitable consciousness, would I begin to learn what happened.

Jim said he started bushwhacking through Hayden Valley about 8:30 a.m. He told me his route, which we had done together numerous times. He said he had just started on his way back to the road when he dropped over a small knoll and caught a dark flash out of the side of his eyes. It was coming towards him. The grizzly drove him into the ground. He had no chance to grab his bear spray even though it was on his pack belt on his waist. This sounded eerily like his first mauling.

Jim tried to grab his spray, but he was face down on the ground with the grizzly on top of him, pinning him down. Jim could not move his right arm. The grizzly took its left paw, slid it under Jim's head, and with one motion tore the upper portion of his face towards the left. Jim did not know this at the time. He just remembered that all of a sudden the grizzly was not on top of him any longer. He glanced up to see a blurry image of a mother grizzly and at least one cub-of-the-year running away.

Jim realized he had to get out of there ASAP! He knew his legs worked. However, he was bleeding profusely from his face and about the only thing he could see was the sun, through a slit in his right eyelid when he bent back his head. Because he knew the area so well, he knew the fastest way back to the road would be along and through Trout Creek. It would not be easy, but it was his best chance of survival. Luckily, he made it to the road at a pullout where the road crosses the creek. Visitors who had been enjoying the vista of Hayden Valley immediately attended to him. Help was soon on its way. He was transported to West Yellowstone by ambulance and from there airlifted by helicopter to the hospital in Idaho Falls.

It took a long time for Jim to recover. He lost all vision in his left eye. His face, although reconstructed, looked very deformed. Although he could hike and drive and otherwise live a "normal" life, he suffered pain and problems for the next three years. Jim died of natural causes in 2010.

I never met another person with as much passion for, and dedication to the preservation of, the grizzly. Each year we hiked not scores or hundreds of miles together, but thousands. We not only looked for grizzlies, but we sought out as much knowledge as we could through direct observation of their habitat. I wish he were still with us. I miss him greatly.

In looking back at Jim's second mauling, a few factors stand out. First, Jim was hiking alone. Second, he was bushwhacking. Nobody knew where he was. His vehicle was parked at a pullout, but that was a common sight. Nobody would have had any indication of any problem until it got dark and his vehicle was still there, or most likely not until the next morning. Third, and most importantly, Jim said he was not making any noise. The lack of noise resulted in the dangerous closeness of the surprise encounter.

Jim was carrying two cans of bear spray on his pack's waist belt, but because of the close proximity of the bear and the speed of its attack, there was no time to draw a can from its holster, much less flip off the safety and release the spray. I don't know if the attack could have been prevented if Jim had been carrying a can of bear spray in his hand with the safety off, but I believe it would not have hurt. Would a burst of spray even as the bear hit him have lessened the severity of the attack? I don't know. It's easy to be a "Monday morning quarterback," but in grizzly country, one's focus must always be safe hiking protocol. As noted earlier, because of what I witnessed during Jim's first mauling almost 14 years earlier, I now carry a can of bear spray *in my hand* with the safety off a good deal of the time, especially when hiking alone and/or bushwhacking.

I think about what happened to Jim a lot. I think about my own adventures bushwhacking alone. I have had a few rewarding bushwhacks, but mostly, the rewards were definitely not worth the risks. Bushwhacking, especially alone, can turn into a very dangerous endeavor.

PHOTO 13

PHOTO 14

PHOTO 15

PHOTO 16

PHOTO 17

PHOTO 18

PHOTO 19

PHOTO 20

PHOTO 21

PHOTO 22

PHOTO 23

PHOTO 24

PHOTO 25

PHOTO 26

PHOTO 27

PHOTO 28

PHOTO 29

PHOTO 30

PHOTO 31

PHOTO 32

PHOTO 33

PHOTO 34

CHAPTER SIX

CAMPING SAFETY

Sometimes when I hike in grizzly country, I will stay one or more nights in order to cover the areas I want to observe. This involves both frontcountry and backcountry stays. I define frountcountry camping as any campsite available by vehicle. Backcountry sites can only be accessed on foot, horse, watercraft, or aircraft. The most important aspect of either experience is proper food storage so bears are not attracted to your campsite. This sounds obvious, but many people have no clue that leaving out food, including garbage, or improperly storing it can—probably will—cause problems. A grizzly that becomes food conditioned, that is, a bear that has learned to seek food and garbage from people and from places where people are, usually ends up dead. Also, bears can become emboldened in such situations and attack people in order to get food.

When camping in the frontcountry, your vehicle is usually the best place to store food. Garbage should be stored just like food and packed out the same as food. To a bear, our garbage is food. Some frontcountry campsites, especially in national parks, offer bear-proof food storage cabinets. Some backcountry sites also offer such containers. Frontcountry campgrounds usually have bear-proof garbage cans. In any case, any attractant (anything that has an odor), including food, garbage, drinks, toothpaste and other toiletries, must be properly stored away from bears.

Backcountry camping offers unique challenges for food handling and storage. When I reach the campsite,

I immediately secure my food, then I set up my tent. All designated backcountry campsites in the national parks I have visited have some way to store food out of the reach of bears. These include food poles, high cables strung parallel to the ground, or a metal pipe set up parallel to the ground. Some of the high horizontal beams have welded hooks. You use a long pole (supplied at the camping area) to transfer your food bag onto a hook. I personally do not like this setup. If your food bag does not have a metal ring or carabineer at the end of it, it becomes quite difficult to hang your bag on the hook, especially in low light. I much prefer the cable or simple horizontal pipe **(Photo H)**. You tie a weight (like a rock or stick) to one end of a long (20-25 feet), small-diameter rope such as parachute cord. Throw the weighted end over the cable or pipe, tie the other end to your food bag and hoist it up. Then untie the rock or piece of wood and tie off that end. Under either system the goal is to get your food bag at least 10 feet off the ground.

In undesignated campsites, such as those in wilderness areas or off-trail, you must find a tree with a suitable high branch to hang your food bag. It should be 10 feet or more off the ground and several feet from the tree trunk. If you are in a treeless area, such as tundra or at high elevations, the best solution is a bear-proof "food barrel." The only downside is that such barrels are rather cumbersome to pack.

No matter what system or method is used, the food must be stored as far from your tent as practical. Such distance is usually at least 100 feet, and in the case of the barrel on the ground, 100 yards minimum is recommended.

When cooking, a minimum safe distance of at least 100 feet from your tent is also recommended. At designated campsites a food prep area is already constructed and its use

Photo H

is mandatory for cooking and eating. When I am camping by myself in the backcountry, I never cook. I utilize only dry food that needs no preparation to eat. This not only cuts down on packed weight because I need no stove or eating utensils, but it lessens odors that might attract bears.

I have had to camp in areas where I have seen grizzlies near the campground. If this is particularly worrisome, there are portable, battery-powered electric fences that are made to place around your tent and/or your food. They are rather bulky and add weight for backpacking, but if you are backpacking with a group or are on a pack trip with horses, the extra weight could provide extra peace of mind.

I always take my two cans of bear spray into my tent. One goes in my sleeping bag and the other is on the floor of the tent right next to me. You should also have bright flashlights at hand.

The best thing to do for camping, either in the frontcountry or backcountry, is proper preparation. This includes preparing for any weather-related problems, having enough food and water or access to a good water supply, a good map, a compass, and letting someone know where and what you are doing. Running into a grizzly is usually the least of my concerns, even though I am thoroughly prepared for such an event. Far more people have been killed from slipping on wet rocks, drowning, falling, getting caught in an avalanche, or hypothermia, than by grizzlies. I believe you have a greater chance of getting killed in an auto accident on your way to the campground or trailhead than from a bear.

CHAPTER SEVEN

TOLERANT GRIZZLIES

Most of the grizzlies that people see or encounter on the trail are what I refer to as "tolerant grizzlies." In the past, I referred to such grizzlies as "habituated," but I feel that this term, as used by most people, is derogatory. It implies that grizzlies may lose their "natural fear" of humans after repeated exposure to us. I am not convinced that grizzlies have a "natural fear" of us. In fact, I believe in many cases that grizzlies have a "natural toleration" of humans, but **grizzlies don't like being surprised at close range—by anything.**

Grizzlies can be tolerant in one situation and wary in another. For example, the Yellowstone grizzly known as "264" was incredibly tolerant near the road with her cubs. In the backcountry with her cubs, you would swear she was a different bear. However, there are reasons why grizzlies may behave differently in such situations. After years of observation, I have learned many things about these, usually, very tolerant animals.

THE BEGINNING OF UNDERSTANDING
Denali National Park, July and August, 1994
Jim Cole and I did volunteer work for the United States Biological Survey (a temporary offshoot of the United States Geological Survey, also known as the USGS) in Alaska's Denali National Park in the summer of 1994. Jim basically spent the whole summer there. I did not arrive until the

middle of July and spent about three weeks there. Our "job" was to find and observe as many grizzlies as possible. It was like we were in heaven.

My first few days involved driving the road to search for grizzlies. It was not difficult. On my first full day we observed 10 grizzlies! I was blown away. I had never seen that many grizzlies from any road, anywhere. We continued this routine for about 10 days. We took some short hikes during that time, but we did not see any bears in the backcountry. All of our observations were from the road. We decided we needed some backcountry data, so we took a backcountry trip and set up a base-camp on the north side of Denali, formerly Mount McKinley. **(Photo I)**

The first morning I looked to the east along the ridge we were camped on and noticed a mother grizzly and one cub-of-the-year moving toward us. She quickly moved over the top of the ridge and out of sight. I don't know if she saw us

Photo I

or picked up our scent, but she was gone. We quickly started scanning frequencies with our radio telemetry equipment but did not pick up any signals.

We spent the next five days hiking the tundra, mostly along tops of ridges. We would stop and use the telemetry equipment to look for radio-collared grizzlies. During that time we picked up two different signals but were never able to spot the bears. The tundra turned out to be as deceiving as the sagebrush areas of Yellowstone.

On the mornings of our last two full days, we spotted bears with our binoculars from our base camp. The first morning I spotted what appeared to be two siblings or a mother grizzly and a large cub. With our telemetry equipment we discovered that one of the bears was radio collared. With that information we deduced that the two grizzlies were indeed siblings. The next morning I spotted a grizzly about three miles away. Once again we used the radio telemetry to discover that this was a radio-collared grizzly and it was a 23-year-old male, a very old age for a grizzly!

Jim and I were amazed that every bear we saw in the backcountry was seen without the aid of our radio equipment. The telemetry only aided in identification, not in finding the bears. Second, we only saw five grizzlies the entire trip, and that included extensive hiking and the use of all the tools at our disposal. Third, finding grizzlies in the road corridor was far more successful than our substantial endeavor in the backcountry. This was exactly the opposite of our expectations. What could possibly be the reason?

Jim pointed out that the only large male we had seen the entire time in the park was in the backcountry. In the road corridor, all we saw were mother grizzlies and cubs, or lone young bears, or siblings. Jim came up with the hypothesis that the bears we saw along the road were there because the road and its human activity provided security from large, dominant males, which sometimes kill cubs and chase away subordinate animals. The food sources were almost identical in the road corridor and in the backcountry. The only difference was the lack of large males along the road.

This was a new way of thinking for us. We now had a base of knowledge for what we were about to see in the next couple of decades in the lower 48.

Glacier National Park, 2010 & 2011
Orange Sunshine—a very tolerant mother bear

Jim and I started seeing grizzlies near trails and roads on a consistent basis starting in 1997. In Glacier this coincided with one of the best huckleberry years we had ever seen. However, the grizzlies we were seeing in Glacier were not along the roads, as was beginning to happen in Yellowstone, but rather they were along or even on the hiking trails. At first this concerned us as we had heard about "habituated" bears and believed this was abnormal.

Over the next few years we realized that this behavior appeared very normal, based on a couple of factors. First, many of the trails (and some of the campgrounds) were built through some of the best berry patches in the ecosystem. Do we really expect grizzlies to forgo these essential food areas simply because people also utilize these areas? Secondly, because many of these same trails are heavily travelled by people, some grizzlies prefer these areas for security reasons just as we saw in Denali. Along heavily traveled hiking trails, as along roads, there appears to be a substantial lack of large dominant males, which younger bears and mothers with cubs try to avoid like the plague. For their part, large males seem to try to avoid people like the plague—perhaps that's how they grow old enough to be large.

So for less dominant bears and family groups, being near people and away from large males makes sense in terms of survival. One such family was led by a mother grizzly I called "Orange Sunshine" because of her fur color. I described the first time I saw them in the chapter "Hiking Alone;" they were the bear family where one cub got separated and had to climb a cliff to reach its mother. The second time I saw them was about two weeks later, below a heavily used trail near a lake. It was about 8:30 on a clear sunny morning. The mother was digging glacier lily roots while the small cubs milled about her and investigated the churned up soil. I could never get all three in the same camera frame because they wouldn't stay still long enough—typical little bears. I'm quite sure the mother bear knew I was in the area because of the noise I had been making. Also, I made no attempt to hide. I remained on or above the trail and did not attempt to get any closer. I was the only person there. I watched them for about an hour before they disappeared from view. I continued to the lake. On my return trip to the trailhead, I saw no sign of them, although I was pretty sure they were still in the area.

After observing them for this second time and this close to the trail, I was leaning towards the idea that she was a fairly tolerant bear. Because of my great respect for these magnificent animals, I felt I needed more observations of this family group before I could confirm my hypothesis. This process would begin to happen in about a month on my very next trip to this part of the park.

I hiked the same trail in the early afternoon of August 10. I had not hiked very far when I saw the same mother and her three cubs high above the trail. They were here for ripe serviceberries. As I stood on the trail, the family of grizzlies started moving downhill towards the trail, eating berries as they moved closer. After about an hour, they were right next to the trail and even moved onto it **(Photo 13)**.

By this time a few other people were also watching the bears. However, everyone remained calm and made no sudden movements. The mother grizzly also remained calm and hardly ever looked directly at us. She basically acted as if we were not there, but I am sure she was aware of what we were doing. The cubs, as might be expected, showed signs of curiosity **(Photo 14)**, but most of the time also seemed to ignore us. Overall the entire family group was extremely tolerant of our presence.

A couple of weeks later I hiked the same trail. Once again, I saw this same family group in almost the same place above the trail. As before, the mother grizzly and her cubs-of-the-year slowly moved towards the trail as they devoured the ripe serviceberries. The cubs ended up on the trail and two of them started to play at intimidating each other. There were many more people in the area. This didn't seem to affect the bears' actions at all. After milling around the trail for a few minutes **(Photo 15)**, the family was on the move. They proceeded down the trail straight towards a group of people **(Photo 16)**. The people moved out of the way and the grizzlies soon disappeared down a closed portion of an adjoining trail.

The next day a small group of us hiked up the trail. It was about 11:30 in the morning. The bears were almost in the same place above the trail. This was beginning to look like a favorite spot for the family. It made sense because the serviceberries were some of the best in the ecosystem. This time the grizzly family came down towards the trail a little faster. They were still eating berries, but it seemed they had somewhere else to go. While the mother ate berries above the trail, the cubs came onto the trail to check us out. The whole family group then disappeared below the trail into thick cover.

Over the years I had seen many grizzlies, both singles and family groups, on or near this trail, but none of them ever came close to epitomizing tolerance as well as this very cohesive family group. In the two-month period since I had first seen them, all the bears were progressing in size and health. I attributed their growth to the incredible food source, which happened to be bisected by the trail. Because of the heavy human traffic on this route, these bears had to be tolerant in order to fully take advantage of the food source and to benefit from the security from large males that the number of people afforded them. This mother grizzly was doing an outstanding job of successfully raising three cubs.

By the beginning of October, the berries were pretty well gone, except for kinnikinnick. The best kinnikinnick areas were close to the road. I had never seen this bear family near the road, but that was about to change.

I took an early morning hike up the same trail but saw no bears. Back on the road, I ran into Joseph Brady who was looking into the woods. There was the grizzly family about 30 yards away, slowly moving in the same direction as we were, parallel to the road. We continued along the road to a parking area where they soon showed up.

We were blown away by what we saw next. The entire family group started rubbing on the creosote-soaked timbers set up as curbs **(Photo 17)**. They were totally mesmerized by these man-made objects as we were totally mesmerized by their actions. It seemed like they were making love to these wooden objects. We watched them for about 20 minutes as they rubbed all over the large poles lying along the pavement.

They then began to rub on an adjacent tree (**Photo 18**) until a man with a camera ran in front of us, towards the bears. The bear family did not panic, but with the mother leading, they quit rubbing, moved through the now vacated developed area, got on another trail, and disappeared to the west. Once again the family, particularly the mother, exhibited incredible tolerance.

Three weeks later I would see them for the last time in 2010. Shane "Mono" Conner and I had gone over for the day to see if we could find this fascinating family. Sure enough, they were about 100 yards above the road eating kinnikinnick berries. We watched them for quite some time.

As they neared a rocky area, the mother moved towards the road. The chubby cubs in their winter coats followed (**Photo 19**). They crossed the road, made their way through some thick woods, and popped out in a grassy area. There they spent some time grazing. Finally they disappeared into thick cover next to a large lake. We wished them a successful hibernation and hoped we would see all four the next season. We would not be disappointed.

I was not able to visit the area until the later part of August 2011. I took a hike with Joseph early in the morning. As we were about half way to our destination, Joseph called my name. I looked back at him as he was pointing to the trail in front of me. To my surprise two yearling grizzlies were happily bouncing down the trail towards us. I had been making noise and looking on both sides of the trail in the heavy cover. Joseph was looking straight ahead and spotted them first. The mother and other cub showed up. Joseph and I backed down the trail to a place where we could safely get off the trail and let the family pass. When we stopped, the grizzly family walked right by us on the trail and then went up the side of the mountain, eating serviceberries as they climbed. After three hours they disappeared over a rocky ridge.

The next morning we hiked the same trail without seeing the family. We sat down to take a break and glass the entire area. There, about 400 yards above us, was the mother grizzly and her yearlings eating huckleberries in an historically great patch. They were visible for about 10 minutes before they moved out of sight.

One week later, on August 30, I saw the mother grizzly about 100 yards above the trail in the same area. I looked around and saw one of the cubs. They were busily eating hucks and moving towards the trail. The mother and the one cub dropped onto the trail and started moving towards me. I still had not seen the other two cubs. It was now almost 10 a.m. and a lot of people were hiking up the trail. I started moving back down the trail as the mother grizzly and one cub approached **(Photo 20 and the cover photo of this book)**. From the photos, you can see why I referred to this stunning mother grizzly as "Orange Sunshine." Her temperament also contributed to the name.

I soon met groups of people hiking up the trail towards me and the bears. I informed them of what was happening. By now they could see the mother and cub coming down the trail toward us.

I told them to remain calm and stay together. We started moving down the trail in an orderly fashion, even though the two bears were not far behind. We needed to find an appropriate spot to get off the trail to let the bears go by us, if they so desired. I now saw the other two cubs quickly descending the mountainside in order to catch up with their mother and sibling. There was no place to get off the trail because both sides were far too steep. We continued backing up. Our group of hikers now numbered about twenty. Beyond us was another group of about twenty that I barely noticed, since my attention was on the bears coming down the trail towards us.

The two lagging siblings finally caught up with the mother and other cub, at which time they appeared to celebrate their reunion **(Photo 21)**. This did not slow them down and they continued on the trail towards us. At this time the other group of hikers started to panic. I could hear screaming and someone yelling "killer grizzlies!" My main attention was still on the bear family and the group of people I was with, none of whom panicked. We finally came to a small flat knoll where we could get off the trail. We did so and the mother grizzly and two of the cubs promptly went past us on the trail **(Photo 22)**.

One of the cubs, however, left the trail and went around us on our other side. Here we were between a mother bear and her cub—a classically dangerous situation. Orange Sunshine showed no concern. It was at this point that the other group of people started running and scattering into the woods like a herd of cats. The bears paid no attention and as soon as they got around us, they started up the mountain into a patch of serviceberries where they ate their way out of sight.

We lingered for a bit and discussed what had happened. The people I was with were very thankful for what they had just witnessed. For most, it was an experience of a lifetime. Many of them continued hiking. The group that was behind us was not seen again. Apparently they ran down the trail and "informed" park personnel of the "killer grizzlies." A few of us slowly hiked down the trail, thinking that the family would make another appearance. Farther down the trail we sat down and took a break. During this time Joseph and some other friends had hiked up and met us.

A park bear ranger also showed up. While I was relating the events of the morning, the mother grizzly and her three cubs made another appearance. This time it was almost in exactly the same place as a year earlier. There was now another photographer and another bear ranger at that part of the trail **(Photo 23)**. However, this time the bear family turned around and headed towards us and started eating serviceberries near the trail.

The second bear ranger apparently closed the trail behind him so no more people would hike up. Both rangers knew this bear family and knew they were not "killer grizzlies." We all stood calmly in one area (except for the ranger and photographer who were on the other side of the bears) and watched them. One of the cubs started playing with a "closed area" sign about 30 yards away and tore it down **(Photo 24)**. The ranger with us said in a sarcastic voice, "bad bear!" Of course, we all laughed. The family slowly made its way uphill and disappeared in thick brush. We continued down the trail. The rangers stayed for a bit then came down and reopened the trail. Once again, this amazing grizzly family displayed remarkable tolerance of all kinds of people and a myriad amount of human reactions. I would see this family one more time that year.

In early November I made one more trip to this special part of the park, hoping to see the bear family as I had the year before at this time. Joseph was there when I showed up. It did not take long to find them. They were in the same spot as the previous year, once again eating kinnikinnick berries right above the road **(Photo 25)**.

After watching them for about an hour, it started to snow. The mother, as the year before, moved towards the road. The family group walked right down the road where they kind of wandered around in the heavy snowfall **(Photo 26)** and finally disappeared into the forest. After about 30 minutes, the sun came out and melted all of the snow. Two hours later the family showed up where we had first seen them that morning: above the road eating kinnikinnick. It would be the last time I ever saw Orange Sunshine.

Over those two seasons this beautiful mother grizzly and her rambunctious cubs taught me an incredible amount. She showed me how intelligent and adaptable these animals really are. She was a great mother that cared for her offspring the best way she could in an area filled with both knowledgeable people and idiots. Her toleration was not caused by people, but was a survival tactic in order to take advantage of the incredible food sources existing among thousands of tourists. She also used the presence of people for safety from the large male grizzlies that avoid humans. She was successful. She kept all three cubs alive and very healthy through two full seasons.

Glacier National Park, 2010-2013
The grizzly known as Panda

While I was observing Orange Sunshine and her three cubs during 2010 and 2011, I also began observing a grizzly we eventually called "Panda." One of the first times I saw this grizzly was in September 2010 **(Photo 27)**. She was with her mother near the road in a thick patch of serviceberries. I did not name her, but the name originated with fellow photographers who referred to her as that cub that looks like a "panda" bear. The next year biologists captured her and placed a radio ear-tag on her.

The next year, in 2011, I only saw her briefly from a distance. I learned that she was "kicked out" by her mother. It is uncommon for a yearling cub to be on its own, but sometimes it happens. It makes survival more difficult because there is no mother bear to protect and nurse the cub.

In 2012 I saw Panda quite a few times and almost always near the road. **(Photo 28)**. This made sense because as a young female she felt more secure where there were no large males and because, once again, there was a good crop of serviceberries near the road. She began traveling intermittently with another young bear that we called Steve **(Photo 29)**. Both bears were two years old. They both looked in great shape. The last time I saw Panda that year she was near the road eating kinnikkinnick berries. We were all wondering if these two young grizzlies, who seemed to have experienced many of the same survival challenges, would successfully survive the winter's sleep.

Mono and I made our first trip of 2013 to this special area in early May. Much to our surprise, we saw Panda and Steve not long after we arrived. They were traveling together between the road and the lake. They soon reached a large patch of snow and began playing. The last time I saw them together was the end of May. They were playing in an avalanche chute at the head of the same lake.

I saw Panda for the last time (that I know of) at the end of July of 2013. She was on and near the road. It was the start of hyperphagia (a period when bears have a very increased appetite in order to prepare for hibernation). She was eating serviceberries. While we were watching she was able to grab a ground squirrel **(Photo 30)** which she carried into thick brush and disappeared.

All of the grizzlies we saw in this area over the years, both on or near the trails and road, during the end of July through the middle of October, were basically in hyperphagia. This provides a logical explanation for much of the tolerant behavior we witnessed. The roads and trail systems are built right through the middle of prime food sources. If these bears avoided people, they could not take advantage of these food sources. Therefore, I believe access to food sources is the prime motivation for tolerance for many bears. The secondary motivation is security from large male grizzlies.

Yellowstone National Park, April and May, 2015

In spite of hundreds of observations of bears in the last three decades, I still have a lot to learn. This can be best illustrated by two events in Yellowstone National Park. The first involved a grizzly mother and her yearling cub. These grizzlies were in an area that had burned in the 1988 fires. It was a great viewing area because of the open, burned forest, safe parking along the road, and a river to keep people away from the bears. I spent three days watching these bears, and I began to see why the mother bear liked this area. There appeared to be ample food, water, and cover—and people were present. I thought she had found the best and safest place to be.

In the early evening of the third day, the mom and cub quickly disappeared into thick cover above the river. After a few minutes, I spotted a large male grizzly on a nearby hillside. This bear started working its way towards the river. He had apparently picked up the scent of the female. It was mating season.

All of a sudden, a car came around a curve towards me. The car stopped and the driver excitedly told me that two grizzlies had just run across the road in front of her. She said they looked like a mother and cub. I felt better. This mother bear had decided to leave, which was good for both herself and her cub. The male was still following her old scent and had not followed her across the river and the road.

I started to rethink my ideas on large male bears. In my

previous book, I had a chapter on these "Big Boys." I related how I believed these bears are very hard to see because of their avoidance of people. It now became clear that during mating season, anything goes. The road, the traffic, and the people provided no deterrence to the male seeking a mate. I recalled that almost all of my sightings of males had been during the mating season.

The second event occurred in Hayden Valley. The previous spring a three-year-old female grizzly bear with ear tags had been seen consistently in an open area near the road in the middle of the valley. She caused many "bear jams," requiring a ranger to monitor these situations on most days. This year, I thought if I hiked into the area before the road opened to vehicles for the season, I might see her and possibly other bears, without having to worry about "bear jams."

On two separate days I hiked up and down the full length of Hayden Valley on the closed road. I did not see a single bear. The next day the road opened to vehicles. As I entered Hayden Valley from the south, I saw a bear jam. Sure enough, it was the female grizzly in exactly the same spot as the year before. This kind of surprised me. I had hiked this area on two previous days, passed this exact spot four times, and had not seen any bear or any signs of bears. Yet on the first day that all the traffic and people showed up, the grizzly showed up. I believe this was not a coincidence. This bear felt safer with everyone around. I believe this bear was intentionally using people to help keep other bears away, and she appeared to be very tolerant. This security strategy was successful. Adult bears, both male and female, and moms with cubs could have easily displaced this young female.

Both of these incidents have given me new insights into the lives of grizzlies and their relationships with people.

Everything that I witnessed in Glacier convinced me that toleration always worked. The two situations in Yellowstone provide evidence that sometimes the strategy works and sometimes it doesn't.

CHAPTER EIGHT

A DEADLY ENCOUNTER

On August 7, 2015, during the writing of this book, a hiker was found dead in the Lake area of Yellowstone National Park. A few days later it was determined that a grizzly killed and partially consumed the 63-year-old man, and the suspected grizzly was a female with two cubs-of-the-year. Of course, the media coverage, both traditional and social, was intense. Unfortunately, this single event negatively illustrated most of the discussions and recommendations in the preceding chapters.

Lance Crosby of Billings, Montana, was reported missing on the morning of August 7 when he did not report for work at the Lake Urgent Care Clinic. A search team discovered his body about three hours later near the Elephant Back Loop Trail, an area he was known to hike. The body was found about a mile from the trailhead and about one-third of a mile off the trail.

A recovery team discovered that the body had been partially consumed and was covered with dirt, leaves, and sticks, as is typical of a carcass being utilized by a grizzly. Forensic evidence, including bear scat, was collected at the scene. Cubs were heard nearby. Traps were set and all the suspect grizzlies, the adult female and two cubs-of-the-year, were captured. DNA analysis proved that the captured female was the bear that killed the hiker. She was euthanized, and the cubs were sent to a zoo in Toledo, Ohio.

Crosby was described by friends and associates as an experienced hiker. He had worked in Yellowstone for five summers. Yet on the fatal hike, he was hiking alone, he was bushwhacking off the trail, and he was not carrying bear spray. Was he making noise? We will never know. Nor will we ever know the exact circumstances of the encounter. Did he surprise the bears at close range? Did he panic and run? Did he even see the bears before he was attacked?

Public reaction to the incident was intensified by the fact that three grizzlies were removed from the ecosystem even though they may have been reacting in a totally natural manner, and because one of the bears was a cub-bearing female valuable to the grizzly population.

There is no law that mandates hiking in a responsible and safe manner in grizzly country. There is no law that requires making noise or carrying bear spray. If someone wants to increase the risk of a negative encounter, that is apparently his or her right. However, jeopardizing the lives of magnificent animals in order to express some personal hiking philosophy does not sit well with many people, especially those that have a passion for the continued existence of grizzlies.

The public outcry over the fate of the bears increased dramatically when word spread that the mother bear was "Blaze," a bear well known to photographers and bear watchers. **(Photos 31 taken in 2004, 32 taken in 2011, and 33 taken in 2014)** However, no one was able to positively identify the bear as Blaze (many Yellowstone grizzlies have a similar blaze marking), and there were known to be at least four mother grizzlies with cubs-of-the-year in the Lake area, including Blaze. Finally, in early 2016, an analysis of the teeth of the killed female proved she was 11 to 13 years old, while the "Blaze" that I and others knew was more than 20 years old. So Blaze did not kill the hiker, and Blaze was not killed by park authorities. Will we ever see Blaze again? She was an old bear. Only time will tell.

Identification of individual bears throughout a single season and from year to year through behavior, areas utilized, and body structure and other physical characteristics is highly problematical. Throughout this book I present many photos of certain grizzlies that I refer to by specific names. This implies that I know for sure which bears these are. In actuality, unless the particular grizzly was, for example, radio collared, I am just making an educated guess based on prior observations. Of course, in most cases I was "pretty sure" of the bear that I observed or I would not have used a name.

However, even if I know a grizzly well (a rather questionable assumption), my hiking precautions are based on the fact that *what we perceive as a safe situation may not be what the bear perceives.* Bears make up their own minds, and encounters can turn ugly very fast. Never assume a "tolerant" bear will always be tolerant. Conditions and circumstances change. You must always be careful, watchful, and prepared to use bear spray.

I believe deadly bear encounters—for the person and eventually for the bear—are too common in an era when technology (bear spray) and common sense (making noise) should make these incidents extremely rare, if they occur at all. I believe it is incumbent on all of us that have a passion for the great bear to set a good example by carrying bear spray and making noise when we hike and recreate in grizzly country. We should also educate people on why our actions are important for the continued viability and survival of grizzlies, so that future generations can partake of the awe and wonder that we have had the good fortune to experience.

CONCLUSION

I have experienced and learned quite a bit since I wrote my first book more than 10 years ago. The one thing that never ceases to amaze me is the more I learn, the more I realize how much I don't know. I can no longer deal in absolutes. Every time I think I have figured out the ways of the great bear, I observe something that I can't explain. For example, many times I have thought I have learned a particular area well enough to predict the presence of grizzlies, only to find no grizzlies when I thought they should be there. There are just too many variables, especially in an era of climate change.

The fate of the grizzly is at a crossroads. Because of our technological advancements we can fragment and destroy the bear population and habitat more rapidly than we can accurately judge the ramifications of our actions. Since I began my endeavors to observe grizzlies more than 30 years ago, the population of the United States has increased from 238 million people to more than 322 million. At the same time, the population of grizzlies in the Lower 48 also has increased, due mainly to the Endangered Species Act, but by less than 1,000 bears. The resources needed to save the great bear for future generations is insignificant compared to the resources our increasing population utilizes, for example, to travel to grizzly country. Our national parks are being overwhelmed and thereby the core homes for most of the last remnants of a grizzly population once estimated to be 100,000 is being quickly eroded. Food sources are still available throughout the grizzly's original range, but because of the sheer number of people intolerant of or ignorant of this majestic animal, the grizzly's future is not bright.

People who hike and/or recreate in grizzly country can help the future of the great bear. Just by using two basic safety protocols we can help reduce one of the most significant causes of the death or removal of grizzlies: unnecessary human-caused encounters. Making noise and carrying bear spray will not only cut down on human injuries and death, but they will help reduce negative impacts on grizzly populations. The grizzly is important not just because it represents what is truly wild, but because these animals can teach us so much. It is hard for me to understand how an animal with such a vicious reputation and one that we push and persecute incessantly, can be so tolerant. Their intelligence, adaptability, and beauty, I think, are unrivaled in the animal kingdom.

In college I took Economics 101. The textbook was written by Nobel Prize winner Paul Samuelson. I will never forget his discussion of the value of things. He asked, "what is the value of clean air" and "what is the value of clean water"? I had never thought about economics in that context. At that time, these most essential resources were free. Most people had never even thought about assigning a value, let alone a dollar amount, to their "worth."

What are grizzlies worth? **(Photo 34)** I believe they, as with clean air and water, are priceless. Unfortunately, many people would disagree. It is up to us, those who love the wild and the grizzly, to educate and set an example, so that our grandchildren and their grandchildren can appreciate and understand the incredible gift that all of us have been given.

A grizzly on a hiking trail in Glacier National Park.

ABOUT THE AUTHOR

After receiving his B.A. degree in mathematics from the University of Minnesota and a J.D. degree from William Mitchell College of Law, Tim Rubbert went to work in the insurance industry where he eventually became disillusioned with the corporate lifestyle. In 1989 he completed the PROBE secondary education program at the University of Colorado. Since 1985 he has devoted his life to the study, observation, and photography of grizzly bears. Tim has hiked various wild areas from Grand Teton National Park to Denali. He has hiked every trail and road in Glacier National Park and most of the trails in the Whitefish Range and the northern portion of the Great Bear Wilderness in Montana. He has also hiked extensively in the Greater Yellowstone Ecosystem. In the last 25 years, Tim has hiked more than 40,000 miles and experienced more than 2,400 grizzly sightings.

During his extensive travels, Tim has made a point of:
  ▸ Concentrating on backcountry observation to learn as much about grizzlies as possible with a minimum of intrusion.
  ▸ Focusing mainly in the Northern Continental Divide Ecosystem (NCDE).
  ▸ Documenting numerous backcountry encounters with grizzlies.

▸ Learning and teaching others about the proper use of bear spray, which he has had to use twice.

▸ Performing volunteer work with the National Biological Survey, observing grizzly bears in Denali National Park in 1994.

Tim has conducted educational slide presentations on grizzlies in Alaska, British Columbia, Idaho, Wyoming, Minnesota, and Montana. He has conducted educational hikes on Big Mountain near Whitefish, Montana, and has archived an extensive collection of grizzly bear photos, along with photos of other wildlife and scenery. He has also instructed classes at Flathead Valley Community College in Kalispell, Montana, on grizzly habitat and behavior. Tim lives with his wife, Suzi, in grizzly country in northwest Montana.

Bears and Bears and Bears!

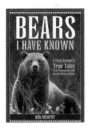

Bears I Have Known
By Bob Murphy

A former park ranger relates his most memorable experiences with bears. These first-hand stories are great entertainment and an inside look at bear management in our national parks.

Great Wyoming Bear Stories
By Tom Reed

The first-ever collection of the best bear tales from all across Wyoming, including Yellowstone and Grand Teton national parks. "An immensely valuable book for understanding and living with Wyoming's bears.
—*Laramie Daily Boomerang*

Great Montana Bear Stories
By Ben Long

Maulings, close calls, and even humorous escapades are all found in these stories, complete with discussions about how to hike, camp, and live safely in bear country. "A must-read for all lovers of wilderness."
—*Missoulian*

The Only Good Bear
By Jeanette Prodgers

A fascinating collection of bear stories that were reported in early newspapers on the western frontier. Valuable historic accounts of grizzly and black bears. "Jam-packed with information. If you enjoy good bear stories, this is the book for you."
—Larry Kaniut, author of *Alaska Bear Tales*